# A Golfer's View

*A professional's look at great Australian and New Zealand golf courses*

BROWN DOG BOOKS

This edition published 2005 by Brown Dog Books

6 The Old Dairy Road
Melcombe Road,
Bath
BA2 3LR

Concept and text by Brad McManus
Photography by Richard Castka
Designed by Kar Heng Goh
Printed and bound in Singapore
1 3 5 7 9 10 8 6 4 2
ISBN 1 903056 18 7

McManus, Brad, 1974-.
A Golfer's View:  A professional's look at great Australian and New Zealand golf courses

ISBN 1 903056 18 7

1.Golf courses - Australia. 2. Golf courses - New Zealand.
I. Title.

796.3523

# A Golfer's View

*A professional's look at great Australian and New Zealand golf courses*

Concept and text by Brad McManus
Photography by Richard Castka

*Contents*

# Introduction
## I'll tell you why.

When I was Director of golf at Moonah Links, one of my responsibilities was to produce a course guide. I wanted to create something unique with great photos so I hired a local photographer to fly in a helicopter over the course and take aerial shots of each hole. The results were terrific. Here began the concept of *A Golfer's View*.

From the sky you can see everything: the size and shape of the green, the fairway, location of the tee, and all hazards. Combine this with ground shots which capture the natural undulations and the roll of the land and you can really understand each hole. Do this for all 18 holes and you get a real sense of the entire course. My intention was for golfers to be able to play in their mind some of the most beautiful courses in the world.

One of the major factors that separate amateur golfers from pros is the planning that goes on behind every shot. A professional always has a plan. They work to their strengths, identify hazards, and formulate a strategy for each hole and shot. I wanted to give golfers insight into what goes through a professional's mind, and hopefully pick up a trick or two.

Finally, and most importantly, I wanted this book to capture the main reason why I play. Golf takes you to some beautiful places. It can take you from the city to the bush, from forest to the coast, from desert to wetlands. Golf courses are built in different environments that introduce you to nature and open you to the elements. One day you will be hiding from the rain under a native tree, the next day smiling in the sun as you watch a bird fly above.

I love all the brilliant aspects of golf: personal challenge, the people you meet, competition, time to think, and so many others. But ever since I was a kid it has always been about the beauty around me and the places golf takes me.

Golf can be like life. We can get so caught up in what we are doing that we forget to notice the beautiful things around us. So step back from the tee, take a deep breath, and enjoy.

Brad McManus

Kauri Cliffs

*New Zealand*

# *Kauri Cliffs*

## *New Zealand*

Sometimes the most beautiful golf courses can be found in the most remote places. Kauri Cliffs is a perfect example of this. It is located in the town of Kerikeri on the North Island and is tucked away on mountainous land overlooking the Bay of Islands. I couldn't even find the signs to direct me there.

Kauri Cliffs was conceived by a Texan billionaire who wanted to leave behind a legacy for all to share. He has a passion for golf, which he expressed here. The course is simply luxurious, from the clubhouse and pro shop, to the food and the accommodation. Then you have the golf course itself. It is so beautifully manicured I felt guilty taking a divot. Before playing, I watched as five mowers cut their way across the 18th fairway in unison. All fairways are striped and the greens are perfectly cut and rolled. It was as if a tournament was on, but this is what happens every day. The money behind this place is monumental and so too the golfing experience.

Kauri Cliffs can be enjoyed by all, from professionals to the Sunday hack. It is tough but fair. The fairways are forgiving and so too the rough. Don't get me wrong—it can be a monster as it is long and open to the elements, but it isn't as penal as Cape Kidnappers or Kennedy Bay. It is the kind of course you could play every day for the rest of your life and be happy. You can shoot great scores and you would never get bored of the views.

The course winds its way up and down hills, across valleys, along cliff tops and through marshes. It has a terrific variation of environments and all holes are unique and challenging. Fifteen holes on the course provide Pacific Ocean views, which are so gorgeous that they can actually be distracting. They cost me a par on the 13th when I rushed a 3-footer just to take another look at the Bay of Islands.

Golf can take you to some of the most beautiful places, and this is one of them.

1st Hole

*Par 4*
*402m*

Drive is downhill so the hole doesn't play as long as it reads. The line here is left of centre off the tee. The fairway is generous. The left side of the green is protected by a bunker and a severe drop. Avoid a pin tucked left.

Again we continue downhill. Drive to the left of the last fairway trap. The green sits above a massive drop behind and to the left of the green. Avoid these areas at all costs. Anything short and right is fine and provides an easy up and down. The green side trap will prevent any attack on a left forward pin placement.

*2nd Hole*
*Par 4*
*403m*

15

3 wood off the tee takes out any chance of reaching the fairway traps. The fairway is wide but don't get greedy, aim at the two trees guarding the left of the green. The green is small and sloping. Anything long is very bad indeed.

**3rd Hole**
*Par 4*
*326m*

The green can be reached in two. Punish driver to the right of the left fairway traps. If you are going to lay up, be aware that the fairway narrows closer to the green and that it is hazard all the way down the right side. Just before the green there is a natural hollow that kicks all shots right, towards the green side traps. The green itself is tiered and slopes from its back end to centre. Take some time to admire the way the green sits against the backdrop of Pink Beach. It is a magnificent par 5.

4th Hole
*Par 5*
*510m*

## 5th Hole

*Par 3*
*183m*

The green is protected by a massive valley short and right. The hole is designed to encourage players to bail out left. Do it! A bank left of the green will bounce your ball onto the surface. The best result is to hit centre of the green and find the same tier the pin is on. No excuse for being short here.

Straight uphill. Drive to the left centre of the fairway. The approach is dramatically elevated so take at least an extra club here. Right is where all the trouble lies. A hill behind and left will aid your ball back to the green, so use this to your advantage.

6th Hole

*Par 4*
*370m*

186m of carry into a stiff breeze was what I was confronted with. This would have to be the most terrifying and exhilarating par three I have played. The view is unbelievable, enough to throw you off your game, but the challenge to hit the green is equally as exciting. The smart play here is to take at least an extra club. The green itself is embraced by a supporting hill that starts from the left front traps and wraps itself all around to the back right trap. The green is large so anywhere on it is a good result.

Kauri Cliffs

7th Hole

*Par 3*
*201m*

## 8th Hole

*Par 5*
*493m*

The hole is constantly uphill, making it almost impossible to reach in two. Play it as a three shot par 5. Drive left of centre, hit whatever it takes to get within 100m of the green and leave yourself a pitch in. The green is narrow and deep. In effect there are two greens here, front and back. The bunkers on this hole are all punishing and should be avoided at all costs.

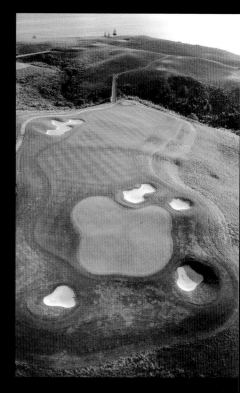

9th Hole
*Par 4*
*353m*

It seems a long way to carry the valley here but the hole actually plays shorter than it looks. Don't get suckered in and try to hammer driver. Merely hit it solidly, find the short grass and you will have a shortish iron left in. The approach needs an extra club. Avoid any left pin position.

23

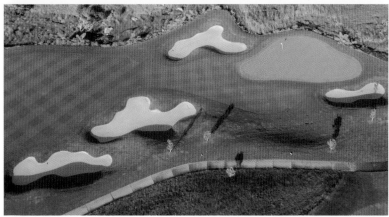

## 10th Hole

*Par 4*
*333m*

This is the first of three successive holes that play through marshland. The marsh works its way up the left-hand side and is definitely in play off the tee. The best way to tackle this tricky par 4 is to hit 3 wood or long iron at the right fairway traps. You will only have to pitch in from here. Distance control is crucial as anything long is in the hazard.

Again the marsh snakes its way up the left-hand side of the fairway. It shouldn't come into play though. Hit driver at the trees on the right side of the green as a hill on the right side of the fairway will help your ball back into a good position. This is the interesting part of the hole. The marsh breaks the fairway and wraps itself all around the green. Any error will be swallowed up by the marsh. You will have to hit a mid iron the right distance to the right centre of the green. Good luck.

11th Hole
*Par 4*
*385m*

The green is broken into two by a middle slope. The front left side of the green is surrounded by the marsh and is very dangerous. The bail out area is the right side of the green. Anything short and left is catastrophic. Awesome hole.

12th Hole
*Par 3*
*192m*

Driving line here is at the right side of the Totara trees, right of the green. The fairway is very wide so there is no excuse to find the trouble left. The green is deep and well protected by bunkers. It definitely plays longer than it looks so consider an extra club on your approach.

13th Hole
*Par 4*
*390m*

## 14th Hole

*Par 3*
*211m*

Another monster par 3. This downhill par 3 is open to the elements and will require a very good shot to find the dance floor. The left side of the green is all fall away whilst the right side is well guarded by bunkers. Par is a great score.

15th Hole
*Par 5*
*498m*

Play the hole with a positive outlook. It is a birdie hole if you can find this narrow fairway. Remembering left is dead, aim towards the left centre of the trees. The rough on the right will hold your ball up if you go through. If going for the green, aim right of the pin as everything will bounce left towards the ocean. This is another dramatic hole that makes you fall in love with this course.

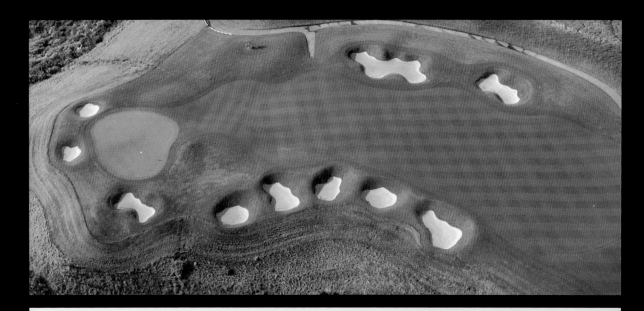

A sucker's hole. Don't even bother trying to knock it over the corner and fly the green (as I tried). The smart play is to take an iron off the tee and leave a full shot in. The green is hard to hold with a half pitch so hit an aggressive pitch in so the ball will spin and hold. Once again the views here are spectacular.

16th Hole
*Par 4*
*335m*

In the distance you will see a bridge. Aim at the left end of it and hit a strong draw. Try to keep it away from the left as the bunkers will be tough to make par from. The hole is long and plays its length. There is little trouble short and right so try to hit a running draw onto this large deep green.

17th Hole
*Par 4*
*432m*

This par 5 looks like the older brother of the par 4 ninth. Drive at the right fairway trap and continue to play to the right side of the green with your next. The green is enormous and there is plenty of room around it. Avoid the sand here and you can finish with a birdie.

18th Hole
*Par 5*
*493m*

The National - Old Course

*Victoria*

## The National - Old Course

### Victoria

I remember the first time I saw the Old Course. I was no more than 13 years old and Dad told me he was taking a drive up to a new golf course that had been built at Cape Schanck. We jumped in the car and headed off. I still remember the trip down the old driveway and turning off a street that led us to the then 2nd hole.

We stopped the car and got out. There was a green that appeared to have no fairway attached to it. After further investigation we worked out that there was actually no fairway and that it was a par 3. You had to hit your shot over the treed valley and on to the green that way. Never had I seen anything like it. I walked around to the green and stood there for some time. This was the most beautiful place I had seen. The view was spectacular—you could see all the way along the Mornington Peninsula and the ocean was just there in front of you. I dreamed of becoming a member there. I still to this day hope that I can call this complex my golfing home one day.

A lot has changed since that magical day as a kid. The Old Course has been joined by two new courses, The Moonah and The Ocean, and the 2nd hole is now the 7th hole. The course features many great golf holes that have been chiselled into a massive dune that overlooks the peninsula. On many occasions you are left standing, happily awaiting your shot, while you watch the swells roll in from Bass Strait.

As a test of golf, the Old Course is perfect. Its location simply leaves it open to the elements. One day you will play a 9 iron to a green, the next a 2 iron. Northerly, southerly, easterly, westerly, you will play all winds here. It is not very often you shoot a 76 and say that you played well. The course has a great mix of holes from long and short, to easy and hard. You learn pretty quickly where not to hit your approach. The greens are undulating and very tricky. You must play clever golf around here. By the way, keep it out of the bunkers; they will destroy your round. The wind has a tendency to blow the sand away leaving inconsistent lies. The bunkers are true hazards.

The National Golf Club is the best golfing facility in Australia. Three brilliant courses, spectacular views, a new modern clubhouse, and situated on the best golfing land in Australia. It is no wonder so many celebrities, successful people, and professional golfers have joined this club. Imagine inviting a friend or business client to play a game, saying 'I'm a member at The National.' The look on their face as you drive in would be priceless.

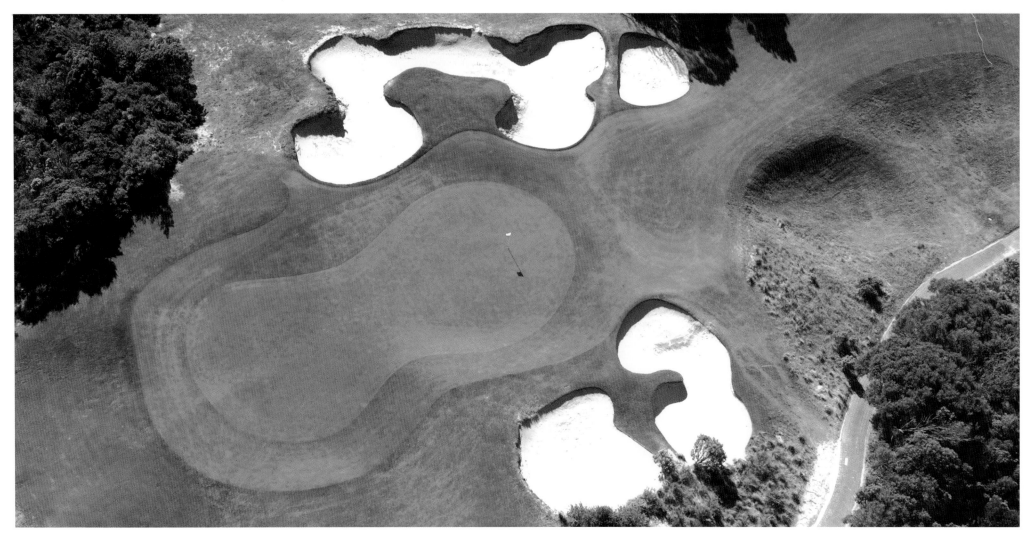

The fairway thins as it approaches the green so there really isn't a need for a driver here. Hit 3 wood just left of the moonah tree. There is a deep valley before this raised green, which puts you well below the surface of the green. The green itself is extreme with three definite sections; ensure your approach finds the same section as the pin. Trouble lies short and on both sides of the front section of the green.

1st Hole

*Par 4*
*342m*

*Par 4*
*420m*

Hit your driver to the left of the fairway traps and you will be in ideal position to make your approach. Your second will be about 150m to a raised green. It is usually an extra club here. The green is large and very well protected by the deep bunker on the front left.

The more you can take off the drive here the better for your next. However, the greater the carry the greater the danger. The best line is to aim at the right side of the furthest fairway trap. The approach shot is straight uphill and can be worth as much as 3 extra clubs if the pin is on the back tier. The green is two tiered and has no surrounding bunkers. Anything short or left will roll back severely. Play your second to the right side of the green and you will get help back onto the green from the surrounding hill.

3rd Hole
*Par 4*
*390m*

This little charm requires a few moments to ponder where you are. Take a look down the Peninsula, appreciate the beautiful land in front of you and then focus on the task at hand. Even though the tee is so elevated it tends to play its length. Play long for safety if need be and don't get sucked into playing to a forward pin.

4th Hole
*Par 3*
*165m*

Aim your drive at the fairway bunkers and play a strong draw. In order to hit the green in two you will need a very good drive. Realistically though, play a fairway wood just short of the green and leave yourself a short pitch. The green has a massive spine through the middle which divides it into two. If you are on the wrong side you will have to expect a three putt. The bunker in front is perfectly positioned and there is a huge valley directly behind the green.

## 5th Hole

*Par 5*
*475m*

This was once the first hole as you will be able to tell by the old clubhouse behind the tee. Knock a 3 wood just right of the fairway trap. From here you will have to carry a valley to a raised green with two distinctive tiers. The back tier will require an extra club. The left side is completely covered by bunkers and the right side has a massive roll off.

Try to keep the ball out of the sand around this course. You will find the bunkers are very inconsistent as the wind constantly empties the sand from these hazards over time.

The National -
Old Course

7th Hole
*Par 3*
*139m*

Ok, this is where I tend to get a little carried away. How could you not though? Surely this would have to be the most beautiful par 3 around. There is the incredible view and then you have to battle the elements to land the ball on the green. I have seen a pro play a wood into this green and a wedge the next day.

The green itself is separated into two by a monster spine. Ensure you hit the correct side of this green. Club selection is everything.

Again take some time out to appreciate where you are. This is the most dramatic short par 3 we have in Australia. This is the reason I play the game. The natural beauty of where golf can take you.

7th Hole
*Par 3*
*139m*

There are not many par fives that only require an iron off the tee. If played correctly this hole will require 2 iron off the tee and then 2 iron to find the surface and leave you with a two putt birdie. Be smart off the tee as there is no reward for extra distance here. The second should be a draw off the right trap. Avoid the left side of this hole and again be aware of the double tier. If you need to bail out then there is plenty of room short and right of the green.

47

## 9th Hole

*Par 4*
*403m*

A strong hole that encourages the driver. There is plenty of room here so ensure you keep it away from the left fairway traps. The approach is to a severely contoured green with a back left tier. Avoid the left greenside bunkers as you will not get up and down from here.

This beautiful hole takes a turn to the left followed by a twist to the right. Once again it is a risk reward hole. I have found it easy to make birdie if you lay up your second to the right place. The green is a double green and really should be looked at before you play your pitch in. Use the contours to your advantage on this hole.

10th Hole
*Par 5*
*521m*

51

## 11th Hole

*Par 4*
*371m*

A blind tee shot here leaves you a downhill approach. Play a strong fade off the right side of the fairway trap. You should only have a short iron in to what is a massive green. There are no excuses for missing this green.

A very tight driving hole. This short par 4 requires a fairway finder. Best play is a fairway wood or iron aimed at the back fairway bunkers. You will then be left with simple pitch to an elevated green. If the pin is front right don't be silly, there is a waste land area to the front right section of this green which will inflict severe pain to your score.

12th Hole

*Par 4*
*308m*

## 13th Hole

*Par 3*
*198m*

Another great par 3. This hole will generally play into the prevailing breeze. It has two defined tiers and is extremely long. Long iron or fairway wood. The ball will usually release upon landing because the club selection you take will keep the ball relatively low. Just find the surface here and take two putts. This is an easy bogey hole.

What I always thought was a driver hole actually isn't. Take 3 wood and hit a draw. The ball that goes too far will be blocked for the approach by the cypress trees that act as a gateway to the green. 3 wood will also allow you to hit over the trees if need be. The green is shared with the 10th and is extremely roomy. Keep it out of the protecting bunkers here.

14th Hole

*Par 4*
*390m*

Downhill, dogleg right, to an extreme green with two tiers. Unless into the breeze, this hole requires a 2 iron off the tee. This will leave you short of the fairway bunkers and with only a short iron in for your approach. The green has a mountainous slope in the middle which creates two sections. The left section is surrounded by deep roll offs and the right section protected by traps. The locals will always use this green slope to their advantage

15th Hole

*Par 4*
*358m*

16th Hole
*Par 3*
*168m*

The last of the brilliant par threes. The green is much larger than you think. The left side is blocked out by a large hill. Make sure you walk over to the right side of the tee to get a better idea of what you are aiming at. Anything far left will find a row of bunkers. If you clear these your ball will kick down dramatically and anything short will roll way back from the green. Land the ball on the surface. It is a difficult hole and par is again a top result.

Another elevated green provides magnificent seaside views here. This clever par 5 can be reached in two if the perfect drive is hit. I would only try to knock it over the left side if the wind was favourable though. Otherwise drive to the corner and lay up left of the protecting row of bunkers. This will leave you with a short iron or pitch to a green that is separated by a spine.

17th Hole

*Par 5*
*511m*

Play a strong fade off the right side of the fairway trap and you will leave yourself a pitch in. The green is protected on the right side by the most penal bunkers on course. Keep it left of a right side pin. Be aware also of the huge roll off over the back of this green.

18th Hole
*Par 4*
*337m*

Laguna Quays Whitsundays - Turtle Point

*Queensland*

## Laguna Quays Whitsundays - Turtle Point
### Queesnland

The moment I jumped off the plane at Proserpine Airport, Whitsundays, I knew my tartan slacks wouldn't see daylight. It was shorts weather. It was the middle of August and the weather was 25°C and sunny. Queensland, beautiful one day, perfect the next.

There is a sense of freedom as you walk the fairways of Turtle Point with the sun on your skin, breeze through your hair, and playing the sport you love around a magnificent resort complex.

The day I played here, I went through the whole professional routine. I started the morning with a full breakfast, followed by 20 minutes of stretching. Then I found my way to the practice facilities. The fairways are Bermuda 328, lush grass that provides perfect lies. I started pitching and finished with a few relaxed drivers. Then I was off to the practice putting green. I had never putted on Tift Dwarf greens. This is the kind of grass you often find on bowling greens. It is grainy, which means the ball will hold up when putting into the grain and roll quicker when putting with it. The grain usually follows the sun so it takes a fair bit of getting used to when it comes to reading them.

Turtle Point is a terrific course to play. It takes you through the forest and into mangroves. Then it introduces you to the ocean and shares with you plenty of wildlife such as birds, reptiles, and kangaroos. It really is just beautiful, especially the sixth hole. You can hear and smell the beach but you can only see the mangroves around you. You walk a little further and then there it is: the sixth. Suddenly you realise you are on the Whitsundays.

The course is very flat as a rule, which lends itself to a pleasant stroll. It has water carries and holes by the beach. A sensational mix of tough holes and holes to attack. It certainly isn't a difficult course, but it will catch you out unless you think your way around.

I see myself coming back here with a few mates one day, playing 36 holes in the day and finishing off by having a few drinks and a laugh down on the mariner. Tropical climate, beautiful surrounds and sensational facilities: who wouldn't?

**1st Hole**

*Par 4*
*365m*

The only danger, other than a shocking shot, is to have your approach shot blocked by a guarding gum tree on the left side of the fairway. Your second will be a short iron to a green that slopes away from you. Land your approach slightly shorter than usual. You should be aware of the firmness of the greens before you begin in order to know how your ball will react.

*Par 4*
*336m*

Fairway is guarded by bunkers left and right and narrows as you approach the green. The best option is to take these traps out of play by hitting an iron or fairway wood just left of centre. The green is shallow and falls from right to left. You need to hit a full shot in to hold the green; it will only be a 9 iron or less.

## 3rd Hole

*Par 5*
*516m*

Pull out the big boy. Avoid the right side of the fairway which is blocked by trees. Fly the cross-bunker and play your 3rd from your best lay-up distance. The green slopes from right to left and has a steep swale short and right. You want to be putting up hill for birdie here.

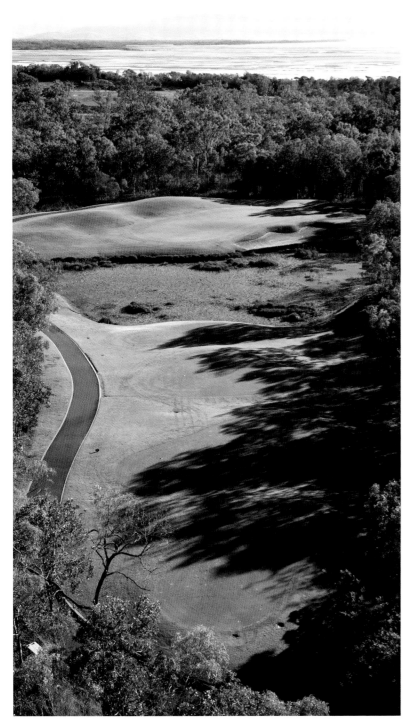

4th Hole
*Par 3*
*140m*

Pretty hole that has most danger short. The green is divided by a significant tier which in effect makes two small greens. You really want to be on the same tier as the pin. Wind will play a factor here so check the surrounding tree-tops and remember which direction it was coming from on previous holes. Better long than short.

## 5th Hole

*Par 4*
*393m*

Strong hole that requires a draw with the driver. Right of centre is the ideal location to hit a mid iron for your approach. The green is well protected by surrounding trees and has two mounds that kick the ball off the green. Aim centre of the green and take your par.

This is great. You walk through the mangroves and probably bump into a few bush turkeys along the way. Then bang! What a hole. Take your time here and take in the great vista. Ok now let's worry about the shot to play. The wind will generally be into you off the water and will try to force your ball into the waste-land bunker guarding the right of the fairway. Find the fairway! Left is dead, right is easy bogey. Back yourself and hit a shot you feel comfortable with.

6th Hole
*Par 4*
*390m*

## 7th Hole

*Par 4*
*419m*

Knock your ball to the left of the fairway bunker you see off the tee and give it a little curry. You will still have a long way in. The green slopes away from you, and there is a fall-off behind the green. Take an extra club as short is where most of the trouble lies. Once again this is a safety hole and the greedy can come undone. Make your par!

8th Hole
*Par 3*
*189m*

This is the fourth strong hole in a row. Bail out to the right for safety if the pin is front or left, and take an extra club. Avoid anything short and left.

71

## 9th Hole

*Par 5*
*475m*

Reachable in two, but it is risky on your second as it will be a long carry to a small target. No matter what though, you must be thinking birdie. Crunch driver down the left centre to provide the best access to the green. Confidence must be high to tackle the green here. Take out the tree short left here and try to be long rather than short.

The fairway narrows as you approach the green, so leave the driver in the bag. Draw a long iron to allow a good line to the green. All the trouble green side is left. This really is an awesome hole. It is a downhill tee shot, uphill approach, with trouble everywhere.

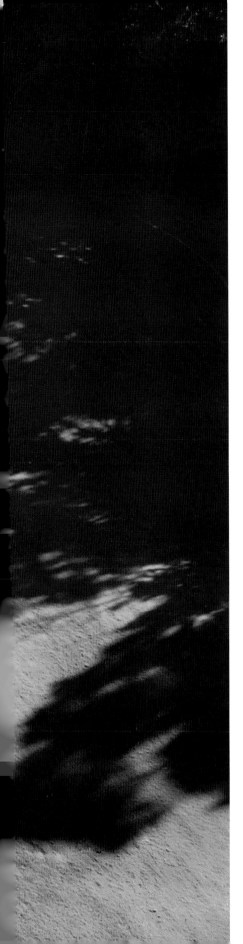

This par 3 leaves no margin for error. Anything short will be wet. Make sure you are honest with your distances and leave any front pin alone. The tee is protected and you will not feel the wind that funnels across the water. The green falls back to front and left. Only a fool ends up with a wet ball on this hole.

11th Hole
*Par 3*
*132m*

## 12th Hole

*Par 5*
*541m*

A strong Par 5. Driver to the left centre of the fairway will avoid the tree right and open up your second. Stay away from the left side and hit to your lay-up distance. The green is tiered and severe so you need to be on the same tier as the pin.

A small funnel between the trees leading to the green sitting against a beautiful ocean backdrop sets the scene for this testing par 3. A slope at the end of the green will save a long shot and trouble, and believe me there is trouble everywhere on this hole. Centre of the green is the answer. Par is a good score.

13th Hole

*Par 3*
*189m*

Once again you are greeted by a sensational vista. This time punish your drive away from the water and get as close to the green as possible on your second whilst avoiding the greenside traps.

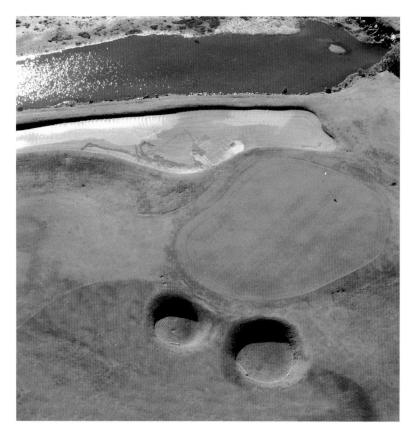

## 14th Hole

*Par 5*
*498m*

Before you drive you must be aware of the tree protecting the right side of the green. Get your drive as close as possible to the centre of the green.

79

## 16th Hole

*Par 4*
*355m*

Position your drive down the left side here. Again the trouble is short but you will only have a short shot in.

*Par 4*
*267m*

Your decision. I guess the question is how well are you playing? I would only drive to the green if I was feeling very confident with the way I was playing. It's still a birdie hole if you lay-up. I think it is an iron short of the bunker and left. Trouble right all the way.

Terrific finishing hole. Tough approach as all the trouble is left and the ball feeds from left to right around the green. Short will result in trouble as well. Hit 3 wood just right of the left trap then play for the left centre of the green. Par is again a good finish.

18th Hole
*Par 4*
*406m*

The Golf Club Kennedy Bay

*Western Australia*

## The Golf Club Kennedy Bay

### Western Australia

One of the great things about Australia is our native animals. The Golf Club Kennedy Bay is home to the most iconic of them all: the kangaroo. These little characters sprawl on the fairways, hop across the greens and laze in bunkers. It really is special. We take them for granted but tourists would love them. Once again, this is why I love this sport.

The course is located on brilliant links land, undulating from centuries of sand being moved by the ocean and wind. South of Perth, tucked away by the coast, it is one of Australia's best courses and probably one of the top five most difficult. It was designed by Ian Baker-Finch, Roger Mackay, and Michael Coate, and believe me they have made a statement here.

As I was taking my clubs out of the car I overheard two guys laughing about how many balls they had lost that day. One had lost four; the other said he had lost seven. I figured they were bad golfers. But after playing the course myself I can understand how they lost so many.

If you miss the fairway you shouldn't bother looking for your ball, as it will be hidden in among the low growing native plants and grasses. The driver should be regularly left in the bag, for Kennedy Bay will eat you up if you are wayward off the tee, and the fairway bunkers have been positioned perfectly to catch out the greedy. The fairways are extremely thin and its greens are as tricky as they come. The course is littered with difficulties. Tiny pot bunkers spot their way throughout each hole. Greens are raised, surrounded by swales and roll-offs, and bogies lie everywhere.

Stephen Leaney said that this was the toughest course in Australia. Huge comment, but I can understand where he is coming from; when the wind gets up around here this place can be a nightmare.

The Golf Club Kennedy Bay is a modern masterpiece. Courses like this, long and tight, will stand up to golf's technological developments. This course is definitely a hidden jewel that deserves further recognition.

## 1st Hole

*Par 4*
*366m*

The first is a great example of what is to come: tight fairways covered with penal bunkers. The smart play here is to leave the driver in the bag and play a 3 wood at the first left side fairway trap. This way you avoid all the danger right and still only have a 6 – 8 iron in. The green is protected by left side traps and a swale, whilst anything right will fall down and away from the putting surface.

Again, leave the driver in the bag. Play a 3 wood just short of the beautifully positioned fairway traps. You will be left with a 7 – 8 iron for your approach. Anything short will roll back into a small valley and left is completely bunkered.

## 3rd Hole

*Par 3*
*162m*

This cheeky par 3 requires perfect club selection. There is a mound between the first couple of bunkers and the green. If you land on this mound your ball will kick through the green to a deep valley. Your approach must land on the surface in order to guarantee it holding. If the pin is left don't get sucked in. The left trap is very dangerous. Play to the right of the pin and kill any bogey possibilities.

4th Hole
*Par 5*
*520m*

Strong par 5 that is a thinker's hole. You need to be smart not greedy. Driver to the left side of the traps and then you make a decision. All depends on the wind conditions, but usually safest to lay up to your best pitching distance left of the large guarding trap. Get your ball on the same tier as the pin.

## 5th Hole
### Par 4
### 419m

This difficult par 4 is called 'Thread the Needle' and fair enough, too. The hole is too long to play safe so back yourself and smash driver at the second right fairway trap. This will leave you with a mid iron to a raised double green. The bunkers on the right are difficult, as too is the roll off left and short. Play long if need be. Anything on for two is a terrific result. A par here is very good. Walk away and compliment yourself.

'There she is' is what I thought when I reached this champion par three. A raised green protected all around by trouble; it is another hole where anything on the surface is a great result. The smart play is long here. The green is 195-metres away, slightly uphill. It sits and basically asks the question, 'are you good enough? Well, are you punk?' I wasn't, I took double.

6th Hole
*Par 3*
*195m*

## 7th Hole

*Par 4*
*285 m*

Tempting little par 4 that encourages you to try for the green with a strong drive. Well don't be tempted—only ten percent of drives will actually get onto the green. Lay up with an iron and leave a full pitch in. The green is shared with the 5th hole and really is a well-protected and well-designed putting surface. Keep out of the dangerous left trap.

8th Hole
*Par 5*
*495 m*

How is your bunker work? If the answer is strong then try to knock it on for two here. Driver to the right of the fairway traps then smash a fairway wood with a little fade to the left side of the green.

There really aren't too many birdie holes around this course so when you come across one you must capitalise.

This is a great hole. It plays as a long dogleg unless you wish to back yourself and crunch driver over the left fairway traps to leave a short iron in. I wasn't stupid enough to do that. I played 3 wood to the centre of the fairway then faded a three iron onto the surface for par. Thank you very much, and then it was off to get a feed and a drink at the half way mark.

9th Hole

*Par 4*
*407m*

For the first time you have a relatively easy driving hole. Play a strong fade at the left fairway traps. This will leave you with a mid iron into a dramatically raised green. The roll offs here are as severe as any on the course and if you find the single bunker guarding the green you are in real trouble. Find the dance floor and you will be rewarded with a par or better. Miss and I would bet you won't get up and down.

10th Hole
*Par 4*
*390m*

Interesting hole in that there are a few ways to play it. I found the safest way is to drive straight at the splitting section of the fairway. This way you take out the danger of the left side traps and there is plenty of margin for error on the right. Your ball should roll off the hill to the left side. Now you have a great line into the green. Right side is very bad and heavily trapped. This is a large green so don't get too clever.

## 11th Hole

*Par 4*
*405m*

You want to open the green up as much as possible here. Best result is to play far right with a driver leaving you a short pitch up the green. The natural swales will kick your ball back towards the green. This really is a good birdie chance.

I have to mention the smallest bunker I have ever seen. It shouldn't come into play, however it is so small I nearly stepped into it. It is positioned to the right of the fairway some 190-metres from the tee. Go and have a look at this little beauty. You can hardly get into it. I stepped into it for a bit of a laugh and gave it a little touch-up with the rake. I think it appreciated the attention.

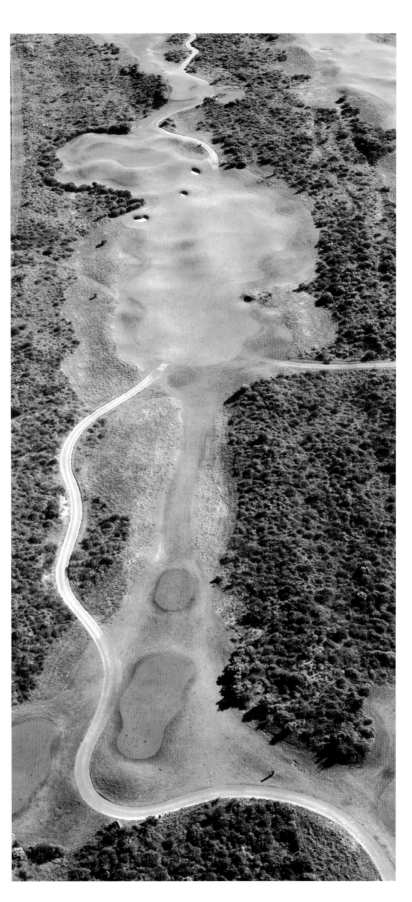

12th Hole
*Par 4*
*330m*

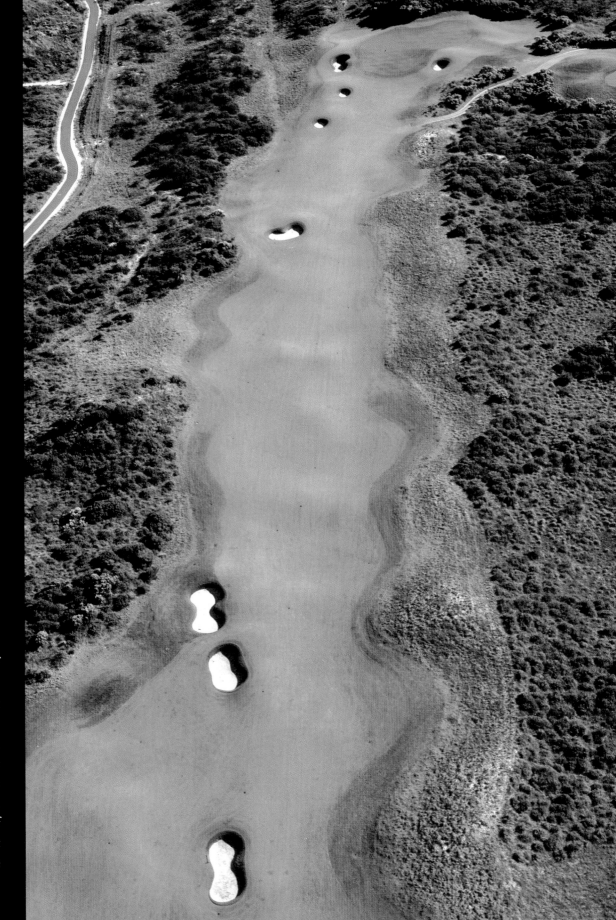

Two good shots will get you there. Driver is the key. Smash one down the right side of the fairway as the right side is protected by a hill that will work your ball back onto the fairway. Now you can lay up (don't get too close to the green as it makes your pitch difficult) or have a dip with a 3 wood. Always play these types of holes with aggression if the danger around the green isn't too severe. Back your short game and make a birdie.

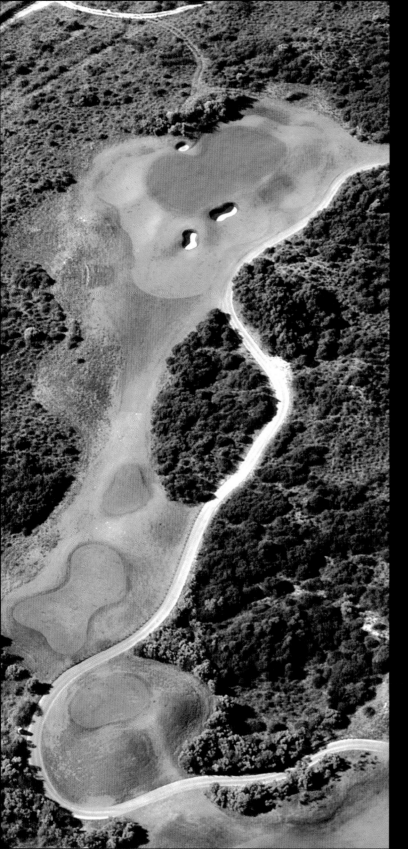

We start heading back in the opposite direction now. Be aware that the wind direction is now changed so distance control needs to be addressed. The green on this par three is beautifully guarded by two traps and the back right falls away to a deep valley. There are basically two greens here, front left and back right. Back right is one more club.

HOMEWARD BOUND

HOLE
14
PAR 3

Use the driver and hit it just right of the right trap. There is a little shoot here that will carry your ball a little further on and position you perfectly for your approach to this smallish green. The green sits in a slight bowl that will generally bring the ball back onto the surface.

15th Hole

*Par 4*
*382m*

16th Hole

*Par 3*

*138m*

All great courses seem to have a short par three. This one is a fine example. The green is raised and protected at the front and back by bunkers. This hole is about distance control. If the pin is in the middle it is going to be tough to knock it on. Be clever here and trust your yardage.

## 17th Hole

*Par 5*
*498m*

Very interesting par five. Do you pull out driver or lay-up with a 3 wood? I think you have to go for it. There is plenty of room around the green and if you need a birdie you should be trying to knock it on for two. If your drive catches the fairway traps be smart with your bunker shot. Don't take on too much, accept your punishment and knock it back onto the fairway as you will still be able to get on for three.

Need a par to finish? This is how to win the tournament with a par at The Golf Club Kennedy Bay. Hit 3 wood at the left fairway bunkers. Don't try to smash it or caress it, merely put a good rhythm on it and find the fairway. You will be left with a mid iron. Centre of the green here is good but anything right is bad news. So with 145m to carry the front left traps do exactly that. Take out the right side of the green and ensure you hit it longer rather than shorter. Be precise as to where you want the ball to land and take dead aim. Believe in yourself and put a good swing on your approach. Bang! You are now on the left centre of the green and have two putts for par.

It all sounds so easy doesn't it!

18th Hole
*Par 4*
*394m*

Wairakei International Golf Course

*New Zealand*

## Wairakei International Golf Course

### New Zealand

A large part of the Wairakei experience is actually getting there. The course is situated between Auckland and Wellington near a place called Lake Taupo. The drive there is fantastic and the scenery outstanding. Wairakei is set among pine forests, surrounded by natural hot springs and adjacent to Huka Falls. It is one of the most relaxing settings for a course I have experienced. It houses lakes, creeks, and a variety of trees that simply explode with colour as the seasons change. And the grass—never have I seen grass so green. It really is beautiful.

The course itself has been designed to test your whole game with a terrific mix of long and short holes. The bunkers need to be talked about. Tree fern trunks support the faces of the bunkers. They look great, until your ball is plugged up against them and you have to play out sideways. They don't look so great after an experience like that. The surrounding trees all encroach on the fairways and capture anything loose. Positioning your tee shot really is vital around here.

I watch the US Masters every year and marvel at the beauty of Augusta, the water, flowers, and trees. Wairakei is as close to that as most of us will get. I have to admit I started commentating to myself out on course as if I was playing the final round. 'Brad McManus the tournament leader. He's got 180 yards to the pin, looks like he's choking down on a 5 iron. He does not want to leave this short Jim.'

Wairakei is a buzz. After I finished my game I had a beer and a feed then I put my clubs in the boot of the car and left them there. Next thing I knew I found myself walking the course hole by hole. Very unlike me, but it was just so beautiful.

The first hole revolves around the drive. It is a relatively easy hole as long as you avoid the bunker in the centre of the fairway. It is reachable when you hit the fairway so pull out a fairway wood and have a go at the green. Play to the side away from the pin so that you leave room for your third. The green is tiered and quite roomy. Birdie hole.

1st Hole

*Par 5*
*474m*

A long par 3 that requires a centre
of the green long iron or fairway
wood. It plays a club longer when
the pin is on the back tier. Take
your par.

111

## 3rd Hole

*Par 5*
*506m*

Fly the right side of the first fairway trap on the left. Stay away from the right bunker. Now fly straight over the fairway bunker in front of the green and you will be left with a simple pitch up the green. It is tough to get up and down if you miss the green left or right as the rough is usually long and the green is dramatically raised.

3 wood will avoid the fairway
traps and leave you with no
more than a 6 iron in. The green
is guarded by grass hollows and
traps short. Long is the safe
play here.

## 5th Hole
*Par 3*
*165m*

The green is thin and wide. Club selection must be spot on here as anything too short will find trouble and too long leaves a very tricky putt.

*Par 4*
*434m*

This hole isn't as long as it looks. The elevated tee sets you up for a big drive so give a belt. You will catch the down slope if you hit it well and will only have a 6 iron in at the most. The green is elevated and has a long roll off if you miss it short or right.

## 7th Hole

*Par 4*
*336m*

Tricky driving hole as trees jut out off the right side. I found 3 wood the smart play here. Hit it with a fade off the left fairway trap and you will be left with no more than an easy 9 iron. Driver will take you into a shallow before the green which may leave you with a tough pitch as opposed to an easy short iron from level ground.

Brilliant hole, both visually and to play. If the pin is back, stay far left. Driver or 3 wood off the tee. If the pin is forward then fortune will favour the brave. Knock your drive or 3 wood as close to the right side as possible as it will allow a little pitch. If you play a poor shot you will find a watery grave off the tee or be left with a very difficult approach as the green is guarded by water.

Wairakei

8th Hole
*Par 4*
*350m*

8th Hole

*Par 4*
*350m*

## 9th Hole

*Par 4*
*394m*

Take driver here and crunch it up the left side. The fairway traps are in play but are shallow enough to reach the green from if you lose it right. The green is well protected by sand. Long left is the safe place to miss the green.

The trouble is short and the hill at the back will stop anything long. The green is very generous so don't get greedy if the pin is front. Take enough club and hit the centre of the green. It isn't a hard hole but there are plenty of bogies here.

10th Hole
*Par 3*
*176m*

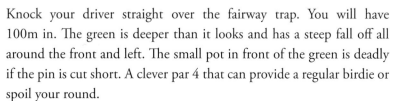

## 11th Hole

*Par 4*
*374m*

Knock your driver straight over the fairway trap. You will have 100m in. The green is deeper than it looks and has a steep fall off all around the front and left. The small pot in front of the green is deadly if the pin is cut short. A clever par 4 that can provide a regular birdie or spoil your round.

Classic elevated tee that forces you to make a decision. I didn't know what to do. Do I wimp it and hit a 3 iron or do I hit a strong fade over that creek. I decided the hole was too short not to have a dip so I smashed driver and had a flick lob wedge in. I probably wouldn't do that into the wind though. The green is split by a tier in the centre. Terrific little hole.

12th Hole
*Par 4*
*281m*

Strong par 4 that requires a well-placed drive. You will be left with a great approach shot from about 150m. This should be played as a draw as the huge pine left needs to be avoided. Not many holes force you to shape your approach shots like this. There is a little pot bunker to the right of the green that can't be seen from the fairway. It catches the blocked shot (well at least it caught mine anyway, bogey!)

Sensational hole. The pines stand tall all the way down the left side. It reminds you of Augusta. Drive straight down the middle and try to avoid the bunkers. Now you have to shape your shot around the huge pine in the centre of the fairway. You will be left with no more than an 8 iron (if you missed the tree) for your approach. The green is magnificent. It is a massive bean sitting on a hill sloping from left to right. It really is one of the best holes you will ever play.

*Wairakei*

14th Hole
*Par 5*
*548m*

14th Hole

*Par 5*
*548m*

## 15th Hole

*Par 3*
*192m*

This par 3 really plays its length even though the tee is so elevated. Easy bogey awaits anything short. As with all par threes here, take par and move on. Hit enough club and aim for the centre of the green.

A blind downhill tee shot with a perfectly placed bunker left and a forest of pines right. Take a 3 wood and hit at the left fairway trap. You will be left with no more than a 9 iron in. The green is deep and if you find the pin back left it will take the perfect shot to get it close.

16th Hole
*Par 4*
*374m*

## 17th Hole

*Par 4*
*393m*

Another blind downhill tee shot that is interrupted by a tall pine in the middle of your view. Punish driver with a strong draw over the tree and you will be in perfect shape. The green here is shallow and wide. You must get your distances right here or another easy bogey awaits you.

The third downhill tee shot in a row. My playing partner wasn't kidding when he looked at me on the 16th tee and said 'It's all downhill from here.'

You can get home in two if you get a good drive away and find the fairway. It is similar to the first hole in that it is an easy birdie if you play your second away from the pin and open up the green. The green is very deep and well protected on the left by a trap.

18th Hole

*Par 5*

*518m*

Royal Adelaide Golf Club

*South Australia*

*South Australia*

I knew of Royal Adelaide and had seen tournaments held there on TV. I knew it was rated as one of the best courses in Australia and I was aware that the legendary Dr Alister MacKenzie was the course architect. What I didn't know was there was a train track running through the course. I had to see this for myself. I mean why would there be a train track on a golf course? I thought someone was pulling my leg.

Royal Adelaide is a course full of surprises. The first of which occurs when you drive in. You see the driveway actually cuts straight across the 18th fairway. I was cruising along with the window down thinking about the game ahead only to drive past a golfer in the middle of his address. I hit the brakes in a panic. 'Sorry mate,' I called out. He smiled and waved me through. This wasn't the first time this had happened.

The course looked terrific, with beautiful green fairways set against dry rough and lovely tall trees. I was pretty excited to be there and rushed around to the pro shop. Then from out of nowhere it arrived. The smallest of passenger trains, just a couple of carriages. I couldn't stop smiling; I even waved to the passing passengers. They nodded back in acknowledgement. What a classic, it would have to be one of the last things you would expect to see in the middle of a golf course.

Royal Adelaide is a sensational golf course. Every hole has character and is unique. The bunkering is outstanding and the greens are tiny targets, many resembling turtle shells, surrounded by slight roll-offs and undulations. The smallest mistake can result in a bogie. It is also a great tournament course that can be tricked up so easily with tough pin positions and long rough.

I felt the history when I walked through the clubhouse. I scanned the tournament boards and saw the names of great players who have won here, famous names. You can really sense the pride of the members and staff. From the train, the driveway and simply the feel, there is something special about the Royal Adelaide. I'm so glad to have experienced it.

## 1st Hole

*Par 4*
*348m*

Wait for the train to pass. Be conservative here on the first. No need for the driver as the green can be hard to hold and the rough is long. Best to play from the cut stuff, so hit an iron to the right centre of the fairway, short of the traps right. This will leave a full short iron that will hold the green. Stay out of the front left trap.

Two strong and straight shots will get you to the green here. The green is well guarded by bunkers, but the left side traps aren't a bad place to be if the pin isn't left side. Keep it out of the right trap short of the green. The green is slightly raised and receptive to a good pitch. Thinking birdie here.

One of the most famous holes in Australian golf. Find out where the pin is located. You really want to be hitting a spinning pitch in here to stop your ball. You can lay up with a long to mid iron to guarantee a safe approach or you can knock driver up next to the green if not on. It is risky to take driver as the rough is long around the green. The green itself really has two sections, front and back. All I can say is work to your strengths here and play with intelligence.

3rd Hole

*Par 4*
*266m*

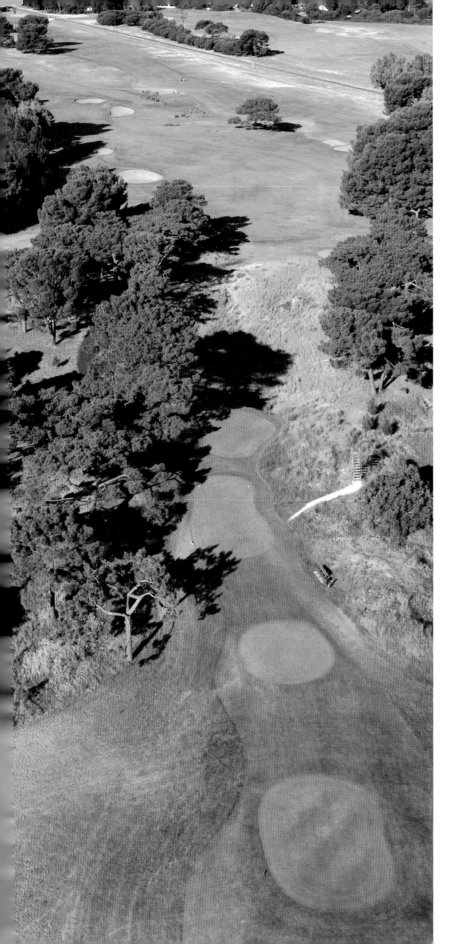

Strong dogleg left with a blind tee shot. This requires a well hit driver or 3 wood with a draw. Avoid the hidden bunkers left and you will still have a mid iron in. The green is a relatively small target that has protection on the front left. It is best to play your approach from the right side of the fairway.

Royal Adelaide

4th Hole

*Par 4*

*410m*

## 5th Hole

*Par 4*
*420m*

Another tough par 4 that doglegs slightly right. The key here is to play your approach from the left side of the fairway as the green is perfectly blocked on the right side by a large bunker. Best shot in is a high fade. Very tricky up and down from around the surface here. Terrifically designed hole that will always test the best players.

Crunch driver at the far right trap and you will be able to play a mid iron into a slightly raised green. The green is surrounded at the front sides by large bunkers. This is the 3rd long par 4 in a row. Centre of the fairway, centre of the green and two putts is how I see it.

6th Hole
*Par 4*
*420m*

Visually stunning hole that really does look like a huge paw print from above.  Club selection is crucial. Need to hit a crisp iron in to a fast surface. Front pins are for suckers, play long.

7th Hole
*Par 3*
*167m*

Not a long hole by any means.
Don't be intimidated by the
shoot of pines the tee shot splits.
The fat of the fairway is the
smart option. The hole has been
designed to encourage you to fly
the first traps and hit the next
wide section of fairway. Don't do
this as the approach shot needs to
be a full, crisp shot in to hold this
small and tricky dance floor. Take
3 wood off the tee.

8th Hole
*Par 4*
*358m*

143

## 9th Hole

*Par 5*
*495m*

Reachable par 5 that requires a long and straight drive at the far left fairway trap. The second will be a long iron or fairway wood that will need to be faded off the left greenside trap. The green has a false front and the right side slopes back towards the right traps which are bad news.

*Par 4*
*345m*

The fairway is split by waste land, so the tee shot must be spot on for distance. Usually 2 iron or 3 wood. Play a full shot in to hold the green here. Your approach will be from a hanging lie onto a green that is shaped like a turtle's back.

## 11th Hole

*Par 4*
*353m*

Great looking hole. It is a tight fairway that encourages you to knock your drive over the traps to a downhill section before waste land cuts across and separates the green. Ignore that option—the best way to play this hole is a 4 iron short of the fairway traps followed by 7 or 8 iron into the amphitheatre. Don't be silly on this hole.

This hole is predominantly into the breeze. It requires a long iron that must land on the surface in order to get a fair bounce. The front left side houses a bunker and the green has slight roll offs all around. Par is a good result.

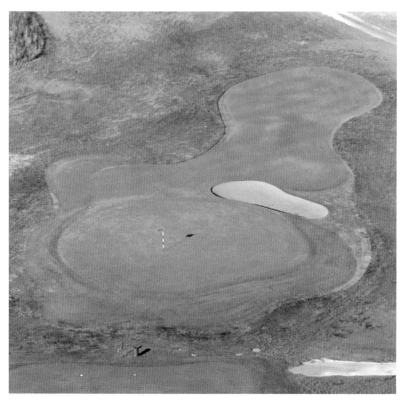

Royal Adelaide

12th Hole
*Par 3*
*205m*

Aim driver straight at the greenkeeper's shed and you will be left with a short iron in. Avoid the left trap that eats into the green. The putting surface is substantial in size for Royal Adelaide and slopes from back left to front right. If the passenger train is in sight, wait for it to pass and then take your shot.

## 13th Hole

*Par 4*
*395m*

The toughest hole on the course. It requires two very good shots to get on in regulation. The drive is tight and the right fairway traps must be avoided. The best line in is from the right centre, yet this too is risky. Your approach will be a long to mid iron to a raised green with severe punishment left.

14th Hole

*Par 4*

*438m*

Thinking birdie here. Smash driver at the far right pot bunker and you will have a long iron or fairway in for your second. Stay away from the left side with your drive. The green has an inviting entrance for a par 5 and should be taken advantage of. The green slopes from left to right. This is not a difficult hole if you get your drive away.

**15th Hole**

*Par 5*
*455m*

*Royal Adelaide*

16th Hole
*Par 3*
*165m*

The green is completely exposed to the elements and club selection is vital. This green is difficult to hit and slopes away from the left traps. The traps are deep and dead. It is only a mid to short iron yet bogeys lie everywhere here.

## 17th Hole

*Par 5*
*473m*

An easy par 5 that is played as a par 4 in tournaments. Let's play it as a par 4. Driver over the far right trap if the wind is with you. Otherwise anything left of the right traps is fine. These traps are deep and very penal. The approach is not easy as the green is raised, tiered and quite thin. Anything short will be kicked into the left greenside trap. This hole is a very difficult par 4 and an easy par 5.

*Par 4*
*383m*

Not a hard finish. 2 iron or 3 wood with a draw off the left side of the right fairway trap will leave you with a mid to short iron in. The green side traps on the right need to be treated with respect as the green slopes away from you here. Be aware of passing vehicles and trains and this should be a very pleasant finish.

The National - Moonah Course

*Victoria*

## The National - Moonah Course

### Victoria

The last time I played the Moonah Course was in a charity Pro-Am. The day was all about raising money for under-privileged kids, so it was a great cause and a pretty good day to play, too.

The course record until that day at the Moonah Course was 71. I broke it (I shot 70) only to watch Alistair Pressnell shoot 67 and take it straight off me. The reason I tell you this though (apart from bragging) is that I was an emotional wreck after the game. Never before has a course made me grind, fight and concentrate so hard over the closing holes. The Moonah Course is beatable, but the only way to beat it is to stand up over the last 6 holes, play good golf and fight. At some point you will be trying to make an 8 footer to save par. The finish is long and demanding—if you have had a bad day early on in your round then forget having a few birdies over the last few holes because it just won't happen.

The Moonah really is a classic course. It features monster par fives and has a clever mix of long and short par threes and fours. Its bunkers are natural and wild and the long native grass roughs add a wonderful contrast to the lush fairways and certainly punishes any loose shots. As I said though, it really is the strong finish that makes its mark on you. All great courses have a strong finish.

When I travelled to the Moonah this time, I stopped my car halfway down the driveway, got out, and sat on a hill that overlooked The National. In front of me was golfing paradise. To the left I could see the Old Course running among the native fauna; below me were the two new courses, the Ocean and Moonah. To the right was the peninsula narrowing to its tip and across the horizon was the Bass Strait. The sun was rising and the natural sand hills cast shadows to define their shape. All around me was brilliant golf course land.

In the future, more courses will be built around here. The rolling dunes cry out for development. The Mornington Peninsula will be recognised as one of the great golfing destinations in the world and the visionaries behind The National can be thanked for getting the ball rolling.

## 1st Hole

*Par 4*
*368m*

Drive straight at the green here. There is more room left than you can see. This should leave you a short iron or pitch to the green which is protected by a front left trap. Generally these greens are firm so be wary of this if the pin is back. If the pin is front left leave it alone and be conservative. This is not a difficult hole but there are plenty of tricks surrounding the green.

A gorgeous hole that swings its way below a natural dune all along its left side. The hole can be reached in two with a drive that carries the left fairway traps, however it may be easier to lay up short and left. The green is split by a shallow in the left middle.

2nd Hole
*Par 5*
*497m*

A driver down the left side of the fairway gives you the best approach here. Anything right will fall off right and leave you with a longer and blind second. The green is long, slopes from back to front, and houses a tier on the back left. It is a very tough hole and one that should be played conservatively.

3rd Hole

*Par 4*
*394m*

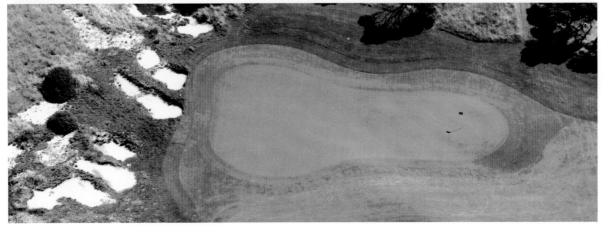

Thread your drive through the moonah trees around the tee and let it fade with the natural contour of the hole to the right centre of the fairway. This will leave you with a mid to short iron approach to a raised green. The green has several bunkers left, so play away from them. The right side of the green is a hill which feeds the ball towards the centre of the green. Use this hill on most occasions. Anything short will be punished.

4th Hole
*Par 4*
*404m*

5th Hole

*Par 3*
*150m*

Left is dead here. Play to the front right of the green for safety. Long is ok as there is a swale at the back of the green that will stop your ball and send it rolling back towards the surface.

Not a difficult hole unless you miss the fairway. Aim just left of the fairway trap and leave the driver in the bag unless you are into the breeze. The second shot can't be left or short. This is a double green, but it isn't a large target. It usually is very firm and open to the wind.

6th Hole
*Par 4*
*364m*

A great drive makes this an easy birdie. If the wind is in your favour let rip straight over the left trap. If not, hit it at the far right trap and lay up for your third. The green is long and thin, falls from back to front and is guarded by a grassy wall on the right (you don't want to end up there). The left side is bunkered and a swale kicks your ball to the right.

7th Hole

*Par 5*
*502m*

## 8th Hole
### Par 3
### 140 m

A short hole that requires a soft landing approach. The bunkers right are dangerous and anything short sends the ball back in your direction. The green is undulating and will generally push the ball to the right side. A long shot will be swallowed by long grass at the back. A tight left pin is very difficult to get next to. Good luck!

This is a beautiful little birdie opportunity. Use driver here and play to the right side of the fairway. The green is lined on the left by bunkers and requires a precise pitch if the flag is back left. Left and short is where the danger lies.

## 9th Hole

*Par 4*
*313m*

There is a windmill in the centre of the fairway here. I love it. It lets us know a little about the history of this land. It is also a great guide for your drive. Hit driver just to the left of it with a draw and you will get maximum run down over the hill. You will be left with a short iron or pitch to a green that is sitting in a basin. There is no excuse for missing the green here as every shot will feed to the centre of the green. The surrounding hills can be very useful in helping you get close to a tucked pin position.

10th Hole
*Par 4*
*374 m*

## 11th Hole

*Par 4*
*359m*

Don't hit your drive through the plateau on the fairway or you will be blind on your approach. The smart play is 3 wood followed by a short iron in. The green sits below a large mound and is surrounded by slopes that will bring the ball back towards the centre of the green. Natural dunes around this green really do make it a visually stunning hole.

12th Hole
*Par 5*
*532m*

You are blind on your drive here, but rest assured there is plenty of landing area over the dune. This really is a true par 5. Drive over the limestone indicator and then lay up with a fairway wood or long iron. The third shot is played to a raised green that is tiered front and back. If the pin is back then use an extra club. Short or anything right is bad.

169

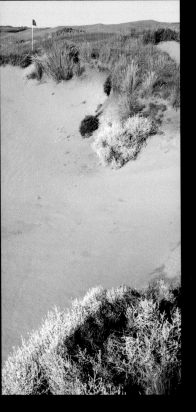

## 13th Hole
*Par 3*
*170m*

A blind par 3. The mounds at the front house bunkers prevent you from seeing the green. The best way to play this hole is to simply find the centre of the green. This can be achieved by carrying the front traps and letting the ball release off the subtle slope at the front of the green. I played one club less than I thought to get to the centre of the green and it worked well.

14th Hole
*Par 4*
*422m*

This really is a difficult par 4. Drive to the right side of the fairway here. The left side of the fairway is heavily bunkered and will result in severe carnage. The approach will generally be with a long iron or fairway wood. The green is raised and protected at the back by a favouring slope, so long is the preferred option. The green is shared with the sixth and slopes from right to left. Knock it on, wave to those on the 6th section of the green, take your par and keep walking.

15th Hole
*Par 5*
*524m*

## 15th Hole

*Par 5*
*524m*

An absolute snake of a par 5. This hole zigzags its way around the rolling dunes to a raised and protected green. The hole really should be played the way it is designed. Driver to the left side, 3 wood to the right side and a short iron long so that it can feed back onto the green. The only way to get there in two is to get the wind behind and cut the corner on your second. I wouldn't encourage this at all.

This is a monster. This is the longest par 4 I have had to play. 447m of uphill nastiness. If you get lucky enough to get a strong tail wind you can actually smash your driver over the hill, but this doesn't happen too often. Realistically the hole is best played by driving to the top of the hill and then hitting a fairway wood to the right side of the green. I hit driver, 3 wood, perfectly the last time I played and still didn't reach. The hole doesn't just bite you with length. It has fairway traps at the worst possible positions and the green is guarded on the left by bunkers that will ensure difficult long bunker shots.

Par feels like a birdie, bogey is like a par, and anything higher isn't that surprising.

When you enter the driveway you will see this brute on your right-hand side. Look away, it will only scare you if you are about to play the Moonah Course.

16th Hole
*Par 4*
*447m*

## 17th Hole

*Par 3*
*204m*

As if the last wasn't tough enough. Here is a sensational looking, but difficult par 3. The slope of the land will force everything off to the right here so aim to the left side of the green. The green too, slopes away from the left and encourages the ball to fall off into a shallow valley and bunker right. The best play is to land the ball on, or just short left of, the surface. It is a very difficult hole and par is great, so if you have to bail out somewhere, land front right and chip up the green.

18th Hole

*Par 4*
*412m*

One last demanding hole to finish with. You will have to navigate your
way through single standing ancient moonah trees on your drive. You
will then be forced to play a long iron into the raised green. The green
is deep, and backward pins will require an extra club at least. Anything
short will roll off and left is trouble. Use the right side of the green here
as it will send the ball back onto the putting surface.

Hyatt Regency Coolum

*Queensland*

## Hyatt Regency Coolum

### Queensland

'Home of the Australian PGA' announced the black sign as I drove into the gates. I checked in at reception and headed off to my luxury apartment to shower before dinner. Hyatt Regency Coolum has an air of impressiveness.

After my perfectly cooked, medium-rare porterhouse steak with green beans and a garlic jus, I finished my $13 glass of red wine and felt an immediate compulsion to return to my room. I had to prepare. I am not usually like this—in fact I am the complete opposite—but my shoes needed polishing, my best tartan slacks needed pressing, and I had to remove any dirt from the grooves of my clubs. The Hyatt Regency Coolum is plush and I felt it deserved my respect.

In the morning I practised for longer than usual. By the time I stepped onto the tee I was so excited I felt like I was playing an event. Course designer Robert Trent Jones Jnr. once said, 'This course is not designed to punish the champions, just find out who they are.' I love that comment. So true too, you can really shoot a low score around here if you drive well and play aggressively. The flip side to that though is if you get greedy and play a poor shot you will end up in the drink.

You see, water is everywhere; eight of the last ten holes involve water. I have always found water courses exciting and at times daunting. As I became a better player I learnt to appreciate water visually, be aware of it mentally, and block it out when it came to playing a shot.

I now understand the Trent Jones Jnr's statement. This course is about risk and reward. You can bail out to avoid the water hazards, but in doing so you make this course so much more difficult. No hole reflects this better than the final one. Water all the way down the left. An aggressive line will leave you with a short iron in, but the margin for error is tiny.

Personally I was stupid on the back nine and paid the price. I thrived on the experience though and can't wait to bring a few mates back with me to play some high stakes skins.

## 1st Hole

*Par 4*
*360m*

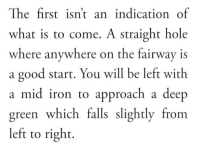

The first isn't an indication of what is to come. A straight hole where anywhere on the fairway is a good start. You will be left with a mid iron to approach a deep green which falls slightly from left to right.

*Par 4*
*348m*

3 wood with a draw will set you up for a short iron to the green. Don't get greedy; ensure you lay-up short of the fairway bunkers. The green is tiered and it is vital to be on the same tier as the pin if you are to have a birdie chance.

183

## 3rd Hole

*Par 3*
*194m*

Strong par 3. Usually plays into the prevailing south-easterly breeze. The green is deep and widens towards the back. Short and right is a bail out area and is easy to ensure par from.

This hole plays its length. Only the brave try to knock it on in two. There is still an easy birdie to be made if you lay-up just short of the green and avoid all the trouble right. The green is severely sloped from left to right. Be smart or be ultra confident.

## 5th Hole

*Par 4*
*318m*

Awesome little par 4. It's only an iron off the tee to the left side of the fairway. A pitch to the green should provide a great birdie opportunity. The right side of this hole is completely dead.

Quality! This green was designed to represent Mt Coolum. The bunker left is the quarry and the depression on the left side of the green represents the mountain face. It really is a strong par 3. The green is raised and any ball falling off it will be tough to get up and down. If the pin is left don't bother trying to get close, play safe and find the centre of the green. You have to love strong holes that also have sensational backdrops.

Hyatt Regency Coolum

6th Hole
*Par 3*
*156m*

189

## 7th Hole

*Par 4*
*348m*

Tricky little par 4. Left side is all hazard. Attack the green from the right side of the fairway. Be aggressive from the tee and leave yourself a pitch to this green. Two sections here; there is a clubs difference between front and back. You must be on the same side as the pin.

## 8th Hole
### Par 5
### 489m

Birdie is a must here. Crunch driver down the left side. If you can reach it after your drive, the right side of the green is the answer. Avoid the trap at all costs, it is an easy pitch from just short and right if you can't get home.

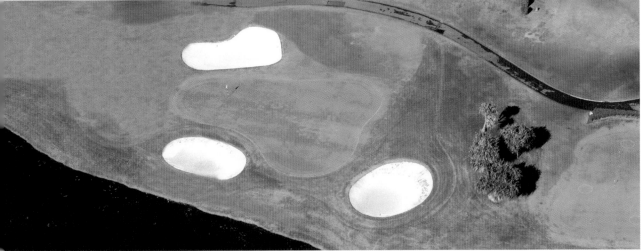

Take a look at the water and appreciate the native birdlife. Now completely forget it is there and drive down the left centre of the fairway. You will have a short iron in. The smart play is to hit the back section of the green as it widens here and you will avoid the trouble protecting the front of the green.

9th Hole

*Par 4*
*360m*

If you are comfortable with driver, punish it between the two traps. The safe play is to take 3 wood and land short of the right fairway trap. You will be left with a mid-iron to approach a long green. The green is separated by a hollow on the middle right. Take an extra club if the pin is back.

10th Hole
*Par 4*
*377m*

## 11th Hole

*Par 3*
*162m*

A classic water carry from an elevated tee. The left middle of the green has a severe mound which effectively separates the green into two. Long and left is the bail out area. If the pin is right, I dare you!

A very tight driving hole. I don't recommend this very often but a fairway wood is probably the best option off the tee. If you play a strong fade and get the extra roll from the slopes you will be able to get home in two. Otherwise lay-up to the left and pitch in. Anything long or right finds trouble.

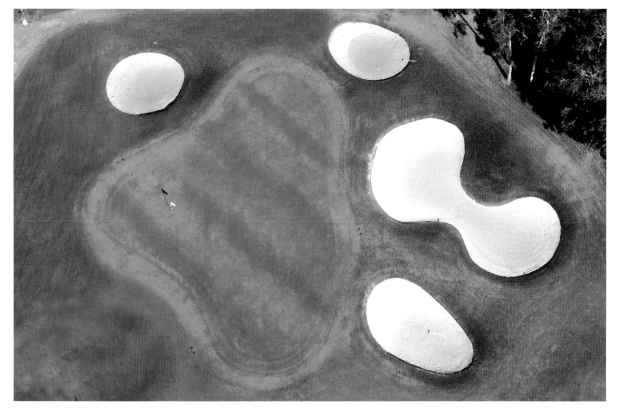

12th Hole

*Par 5*
*479m*

195

## 13th Hole

*Par 4*
*361m*

The braver you are here the easier the hole becomes. The best line from the tee is right of the green side bunker. This should leave you a short iron in. The approach is uphill to a two tiered green. There is water on the right and sand left. No margin for error here. Long and left is the safe spot.

Water again protects this green. The green has a dramatic contour from right to left which should feed your ball to the centre of the green. Don't let the water come into play. Short and right is a safe option.

14th Hole

*Par 3*
*187m*

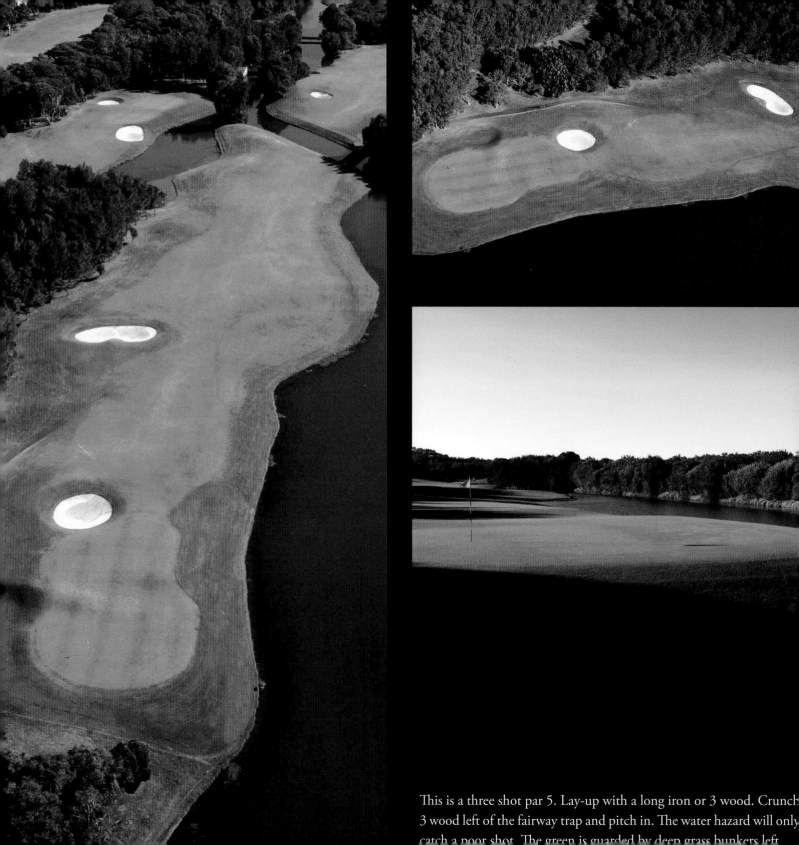

This is a three shot par 5. Lay-up with a long iron or 3 wood. Crunch
3 wood left of the fairway trap and pitch in. The water hazard will only
catch a poor shot. The green is guarded by deep grass bunkers left

Love this hole. It's a short par 4, easily birdieable, that sits against the incredible backdrop of Mt Coolum. It is a long iron or 3 wood from the tee. Aim just left of the first fairway bunker. This should leave you with a short pitch to an elevated and small target. It is a birdie hole but can kill your round.

16th Hole

*Par 4*

*324m*

Fly the traps. You will have a pitch to an elevated green. The green slopes from back to front which means you need to be putting up the hill for birdie. Yardages are vital here as anything short will roll a long way back whilst being above the hole leaves you with a scary putt.

17th Hole

*Par 4*
*369m*

What a finish. This will test your nerve. Must back yourself here. Imagine needing to make a birdie to win the Australian PGA. The pin is back left which is surrounded by water. You want to be hitting as short a club as possible on your approach. So drive the ball at the left side of the second fairway trap. Aim your approach just right of the pin and let it feed to the hole. Great courses always have a strong finishing hole and this is one of the best.

18th Hole
*Par 4*
*390m*

*tional - Moonah Course, Kauri Cliffs, The Golf Club Kennedy Bay, Wairakei, Royal Adelaide Golf Course, Hyatt Coolum*

Cape Kidnappers

*New Zealand*

## Cape Kidnappers

### New Zealand

I was told that Cape Kidnappers was breathtaking but I still wasn't prepared. I had no idea a golf course could be built in a location like this. Cape Kidnappers must be one of the most dramatic golf courses in the world.

The drive through Clive and other surrounding suburbs gives you no clue as to what you will encounter. The journey of Cape Kidnappers really begins at the entrance of the eight-kilometre driveway which winds its way along creeks, over ravines, through forests and past sheep stations. Finally you arrive at the clubhouse, which is quite small and has been built to capture the character of the place. The clubhouse intentionally symbolises an old sheep shed. You see, this is old farming land that has been turned into the most magnificent golf course I have ever seen. Course designer Tom Doak has left the land's natural flow and merely placed tees, greens and bunkers.

Playing this course is a gargantuan task. The front nine holes work their way around old farm fields behind the clubhouse and challenge all facets of your game. The fairways are generous and the greens are large and undulating, but fair. The trouble is found in the perfectly placed fairway bunkers and long fescue roughs. Anything off the fairways is severely punished or lost. The course is heavily influenced by weather elements and can only be classed as extremely difficult.

The back nine takes you to places golfers have never imagined. Greens on the side of 140-metre cliffs, tees isolated on slits of mountain and ball carries over enormous valleys. The views of the cliff faces and beautiful Hawks Bay add to the greatest golfing experience of your life.

Don't come here expecting to shoot your best score. Come here to appreciate the personal challenge, natural beauty, and sensational holes. The whole experience from the drive up, to the friendly staff, and to playing the course is a complete golfer's heaven. Every passionate golfer must take on the adventure that is Cape Kidnappers.

## 1st Hole

*Par 4*
*402m*

Strong opening par 4. A deep gully separates the green from the fairway. The line is left centre of the fairway to avoid the fairway traps. Driver is the play here and you should be left with a 5 to 9 iron for your approach. Anything left of the green is desperate trouble so play safe to the right section of the green and a safe par can be made. The green is tiered and slopes from right to left.

206

Drive over the left side of the fairway traps. You can get home with a strongly faded fairway wood for your second. If not in range, lay up to the left side of the fairway, short of the right traps. There are not many birdies on this course, this can be one of them.

The front right traps look greenside, however there is at least a 10 metre gap between them and the green. This provides a perfect landing area as the roll of the land will deflect the ball onto the green. It is a long iron or fairway wood to reach the green on the fly. Stay away from a left pin placement.

4th Hole
*Par 5*
*497m*

The drive is blind. The fairway is generous though so play a strong draw just to the left of the direction marker and you will receive extra run down the hill. The next approach is a classic. If you can reach it in two play it to the left side of the green. Don't mess with the right as you will have to reload. The green is deep and severely tiered. The slope in the middle will roll your ball back to the front portion. The safe place here is long and left.

## 5th Hole

*Par 4*
*384m*

Anything short will roll back a long way as a deep gully protects the green. Take an extra club if the pin is forward. Fairway traps force a decision. 3 wood at the far right fairway traps is the correct play unless the wind is in your favour, then a drive down the left will allow a shorter approach to the green.

Unbelievably difficult. You won't find your ball if you miss left. The play is for complete safety. Hit to the right side of the green. The carry seems to play longer so take an extra club. This green is huge so try to lag your putt as close as you can. Par is a brilliant result.

6th Hole

*Par 3*
*206m*

**7th Hole**

*Par 4*
*414m*

Play to the top level of this fairway. There is no benefit hitting into the dropping fairway, so 3 wood probably is the best play downwind. A tough approach with no margin for error. Centre of the green is the best play as a false front will send your ball way back into the valley.

This hole plays over a valley of trees so short is bad news. The green is tiered with a slope funneling down to the front. If the pin is forward use the slope to your advantage, hit the ball just past the pin and it will feed back to the pin. It is a good idea to hit an extra club here.

8th Hole
*Par 3*
*166m*

The only safe miss is right.

## 9th Hole
*Par 4*
*369m*

Drive towards the clubhouse as hidden fairway bunkers protect the right. The green sits above a massive valley and slopes from back right to the front left. Once again, long is the safe play and avoid the left at all costs. If you do end up in the long fescue roughs you might bump into one of the local pheasants.

A long par 4 that lends to a right of centre drive. The approach can be played by running the ball onto the green from right to left. Play long if possible as anything left will feed into the traps, long rough or a deep valley. The green is generous and a par is again a great score.

**11th Hole**

*Par 3*
*205m*

This course just doesn't let up. This is another difficult par 3, with left of the green being completely dead. The green is very narrow in the front, deep and undulating. You have to thread the needle here to find the surface. Play your long iron or fairway wood to the back right side of the green.

12th Hole
*Par 4*
*421m*

This is a huge fairway so hammer your drive. The reason for this is to allow as short an iron in as possible for your approach. The green sits against the horizon with deep fall offs on both sides. Long is the smart play here as the next tee hides behind the green and protects your ball from danger. The target looks small against the ocean backdrop but is in fact quite large.

## 13th Hole

*Par 3*
*119m*

A tiny hole that is enormous in stature. The green is very difficult to hold, especially short. Deep bunkers await both sides. Aim for the back middle of the green.

Sensational hole. Drive left of where you think the line is, as the valley right is there to catch any hint of fade. The green is protected by the sneakiest bunker of all. It prevents most attacks at the pin. The green is extremely narrow and has a false front right and a run off at the back. The best way to play the hole is to leave a full wedge or sand iron approach that should be aimed left of the pot bunker.

15th Hole
*Par 5*
*594m*

Oh my god! The longest and scariest par 5 ever. The hole runs out along a shaft of ground on top of a 140m high cliff. The green itself seems to get further away as you approach it. This hole requires three long straight shots to reach it in regulation. If you miss the fairway the chances are you will lose your ball. The green is small and if you are long by two meters your ball disappears into the ocean below. Try to keep your shots low. It is the most dramatic hole on the course.

15th Hole
*Par 5*
*594m*

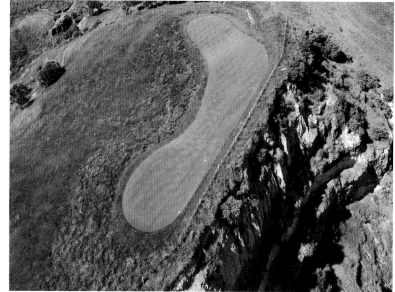

I stood on the tee for ten minutes just taking in the view. I really wanted to lay down a picnic rug, open a bottle of red and spend the rest of the day there. Seagulls fly around below as you stand 140m above the ocean. It's special.

When it is time to play the hole, pull out your driver and drive with reckless abandon. Use the scenery for inspiration and hit the drive of your life. (This is highly unprofessional but it doesn't matter at this stage, you will feel alive and well, and just ecstatic that you play this game.)

The fairway narrows where the ball lands so it has to be straight. Take one more look behind you, for you will remember this teeing ground forever, and head off. Your second shot is uphill to a beautifully bunkered green. Avoid the right side as the bunkers are tough.

16th Hole

*Par 5*
*457m*

## 17th Hole

*Par 4*
*423m*

This hole requires two great shots to get home in regulation. Smash driver and you still have a long uphill second over a gathering of bunkers. You can bail out right if need be but the best result is to fly the traps. The green slopes from back left to right.

## 18th Hole
*Par 4*
*439m*

A difficult drive here. Stay away from the left side. You will have another long approach to a green that sits in a bowl to the right of the fairway. Left of the green is a hill that will take your ball onto the surface but try to land it flush on the green for the best result.

New South Wales Golf Club

*New South Wales*

## New South Wales Golf Club

### New South Wales

I had to play at NSW Golf Club purely for one reason: the 5th and 6th holes. Nowhere in Australia are there two more photographed holes. On the 6th you find yourself standing on a rock island, hitting over the rock pools and crystal blue water. You can see fish and sea life all around you. I wasn't sure if I wanted to play golf or go fishing! I found myself wishing I had brought my flippers and snorkel. But the course doesn't end with just the 5th and 6th: the entire golf complex is beautiful and really is the complete package.

The NSW Golf Club is set amongst national park in La Perouse and is located at Cape Banks on the headland of Botany Bay. It is a coastal course with rare views that inspire. The course flows through, along, and around the natural dunes. It demands creative shot making and will test the resolve of all players. The bunkering is brilliant and trouble awaits any loose shot. The fairways are quite narrow at times and the lies in the rough will punish. The course has been the host to several professional events and is truly a championship course.

My experience was one of relaxation as I wandered slowly from tee to green, stopping from time to time to watch a passing ship or crashing wave. Sydney sits in the background and forms a classic silhouette on the horizon.

I found myself wondering if the old captain saw the potential of this land. I can imagine Captain Cook searching through his telescope and turning to his crew and saying 'I tell you what boys, I think we should drop anchor just off the coast over there. Go below deck and grab your clubs because we are going to row ourselves to that rock to play a few holes. I believe that is the perfect place for a golf course. Who is with me? Make sure you bring a few extra balls, it looks a little rugged.'

What a great man, what a great place, what a great sport!

**1st Hole**

*Par 4*
*293m*

Inviting isn't it? Only 290 metres to the green. Well, be smart folks for this little baby can jump up and rip your heart out on the first shot. This is an easy hole if you pull out a 2 iron and find the fairway. This will eliminate any danger and leave a simple uphill pitch to a green that slopes from back to front. This may seem conservative, but only a fool takes a risk with their first shot.

Lovely strong par 3. The green sits up high and angles 45 degrees at you. The green is broken into two sections by clever central run offs, so club selection is vital and so too is not going through the green. Try to land the ball on the same section as the pin. Two bunkers protect the back left side of the green. This is a difficult hole early on. Definitely play for a par.

Par 4 dogleg left to a raised green that encourages the ball to roll centrally. Is it hard? The answer is no. It really doesn't play as long as the yardage suggests, yet it can be a danger. Risk and reward. Driver will leave you with an easy approach however it also increases the risk of a bogie. I think it is merely a well struck 3 wood with a draw followed by a mid to short iron up the hill. Make this an easy hole and walk away with a par.

3rd Hole

*Par 4*
*380m*

## 4th Hole
*Par 4*
*391m*

Hit driver straight down the right side of the fairway. Keep the left-hand side out of play here. The fairway is quite skinny and the rough isn't usually too thick. The green slopes from left to right and back to front. I recommend coming in from the right side to open up the green and make it easier to hold the green.

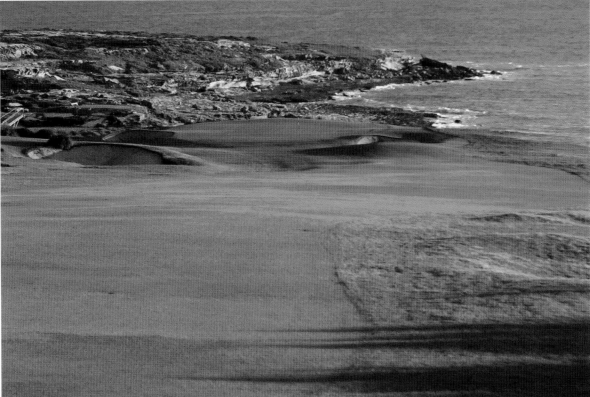

5th Hole

*Par 5*
*468m*

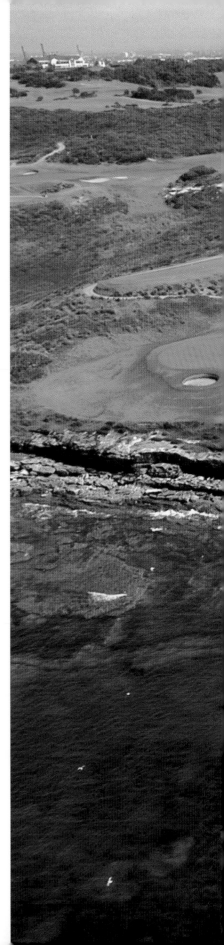

This is one of the most celebrated holes in Australian golf. So enjoy the challenge, but more importantly enjoy the views.

## 5th Hole

*Par 5*
*468m*

The hole itself all comes down to the success of the drive. It is 230m to the top of the hill and 260m to reach the down slope. Obviously, wind conditions play a huge part. Be clever if you can't reach the green in two. Lay up to the right side of the fairway so you can open up the green. There is a guarding trap some 20m short and left of the green, which you need to ensure doesn't come into play.

It really is a personal high when you get to the top of the hill and look down to the green set short of the amazing ocean view. What a fantastic place to build a golf course. This really is a wonderful place to play. Lucky members!

The approach is uphill, which will generally add another club to your selection, and the green falls off towards the water. Anywhere on the green is good, but ideally you want to leave yourself an uphill putt, so the left side of the green is preferred. I hit 4 iron to the heart, then rolled in a 15 footer for birdie. Bang! Take that. I just birdied the 2 most recognised holes in Sydney if not Australia.

6th Hole
*Par 3*
*177m*

## 7th Hole

*Par 4*
*376m*

Straight uphill. Play your drive straight down the middle. There is a natural concave here which will help you find the surface. Your next will be to a raised green which slopes from back to front and has a little mound on the front left side. Take an extra club and try to avoid this mounded area. The hole has a natural feel as you walk away from the ocean and through the weathering dunes on the right.

This hole is a great example of the narrow fairways around this course. Drive long and with fury to get as close to the fairway break as possible. Now you probably won't get there so hit 3 wood to the left side of the fairway and open up the green. The right side of this green is very difficult to get up and down from so avoid it completely. The back of the green is surrounded by a grassy hill; once again you do not want to be in there.

## 9th Hole

*Par 4*
*340m*

Unique little hole this one. Play a 3 wood with a fade here to hold against the natural contour of the fairway. This will leave a pitch into the funkiest green I have ever seen. Short is the best option here if the pin is back. Anything over the back is dead. It really is difficult to get up and down from anywhere off the surface. Not a hard hole so be smart with your approach.

10th Hole
*Par 4*
*360m*

Aim driver just right of the left fairway trap and hit a strong, running fade. This will avoid the trouble left and leave a relatively easy approach with a short iron. The green is well protected on the right by traps, and slopes with the hill from left to right. The green widens as it deepens. The safe spot is back. Don't miss it in the left traps here either as they look simple to play from, but are actually easy bogey material. Terrific green, it really does make the hole.

241

Short and sweet. This hole has a strange character. The green sits in the middle of nowhere and is surrounded by small deep traps. It leans towards the tee except for the back section which runs off. Always play to the safe side of the flag. You don't want to go long here. It is inviting to attack the flag here if it is short. Just be aware.

11th Hole

*Par 3*
*149m*

A tight driving hole with waste land left and bushes right. Back yourself, fly the hill and you will be able to knock it on for two. The green is brilliantly designed. It has a narrow mouth and widens as it gets deeper. The bunkers either side will usually catch the second shot in. However, I encourage you to play into the right side traps if you are confident with your sandmanship.

12th Hole
*Par 5*
*482m*

Hit driver here onto the fairway and you will only have a short iron in. The natural contours will aid your ball if you play a draw off the right-hand side. Long and right or short left are no good.

13th Hole

*Par 4*
*375m*

14th Hole
*Par 4*
*323m*

This is outstanding course design. We really are playing around the sides of the hills now. This sort of dogleg left requires a good drive straight to the heart of the fairway. The fairway itself is concave so anything long will roll back onto the cut grass. Keep away from the left side here. The approach is to an unbunkered green that is surrounded by bush. If you go long and left you may have to reload.

245

## 15th Hole
*Par 4*
*372m*

The drive requires 205m of carry to get to the top of the rise, so it may be a 3 wood. Keep away from the right side here or you will be blocked for your approach to the green. The downhill approach should only be a mid to short iron. The green has a false front and a swale on its left side. Back right is a grassy hole which acts as a good bail out area.

The final leg of sensational twisting holes across sloping ground. This is a tough driving hole that bends to the left and works its way to a bean-shaped green guarded left by three tiny bunkers and surrounded right by a natural hill. Avoid the bunkers left and play to the right centre of the green. The green slopes with the hill and anything long is caught up in long grass at the back of the green.

16th Hole

*Par 4*

*403m*

The tee and green are perched on top of a ridge and are open to the elements. The green is narrow at the front and has a severe drop off back right. It is a small target and should be treated with complete respect. The wind will play a monster role here.

18th Hole

*Par 5*
*501m*

I was so surprised by the last hole here. It is a flat hole with no trees that looks boring and completely out of character with the rest of the course. At least I thought that before I played it. Then I discovered the fairway steps up to the green. Two good shots will get you close and birdie should be made. It has a strange feel and the green design is very clever. It adds to the wonder of this amazing golf course.

## Kauri Cliffs, *New Zealand*

Kauri Cliffs, Matauri Bay Road,
Northland, New Zealand
Tel: + 64 9 405 1900
Fax: + 64 9 407-0061
Website: www.kauricliffs.com

## The National - Old Course, *Victoria*

10 The Cups Drive
Cape Schanck, Victoria 3939
Tel: +61 (0)3 5988 6666
Fax: +61 (0)3 5988 6744
Website: www.nationalgolf.com.au

## Laguna Quays Whitsundays - Turtle Point, *Queensland*

Kunapipi Springs Road
Midge Point, Whitsundays
Queensland 4799
Tel: + 61 (0)7 4947 7777
Fax: + 61 (0)7 4947 7770
Website: www.lagunawhitsundays.info

## The Golf Club Kennedy Bay, *Western Australia*

Port Kennedy Drive
Port Kennedy, Western Australia 6172
Tel: +61 (0)8 9524 5333
Fax: +61 (0)8 9524 5444
Website: www.thegolfclub.com.au

## Wairakei International Golf Course, *New Zealand*

State Highway One, PO Box 377
Taupo 2730
New Zealand
Tel: +64 7 374 8152
Fax: +64 7 374 8289
Website: www.wairakeigolfcourse.co.nz

Royal Adelaide Golf Course, *South Australia*
328 Tapleys Hill Road
Seaton, Adelaide, South Australia 5023
Tel: + 61 (0)8 8356 5511
Fax: + 61 (0)8 8235 1064
Website: www.royaladelaidegolf.com.au

The National - Moonah Course, *Victoria*
10 The Cups Drive
Cape Schanck, Victoria 3939
Tel: + 61 (0)3 5988 6666
Fax: + 61 (0)3 5988 6744
Website: www.nationalgolf.com.au

Hyatt Regency Coolum, *Queensland*
Warren Road
Coolum Beach, Queensland 4573
Tel: + 61 (0)7 5446 1234
Fax: + 61 (0)7 5446 2957
Website: http://coolum.regency.hyatt.com

Cape Kidnappers, *New Zealand*
448 Clifton Road
Te Awanga, Hawke's Bay
Tel: + 64 6 875 1900
Fax: + 64 6 875 1901
Website: www.capekidnappers.com

New South Wales Golf Course, *New South Wales*
Henry Head Road
La Perouse, Sydney, New South Wales 2000
Tel: +  61 (0)2 9661 4455
Fax: + 61 (0)2 9311 3792
Website: www.nswgolfclub.com.au

*Club details*

# Brad McManus

Brad McManus grew up in Melbourne, Australia and was educated at Camberwell Grammar School. He began his golfing career at the Portsea G.C. under mentor Bill Branthwaite and later completed a traineeship at the Sorrento G.C. under the guidance of Brett Parker.

A qualified PGA member, he moved to Moonah Links and later became Director of Golf, just in time for Moonah Links' first Australian Open in 2003.

⤙

Can I just say this project has been the most enjoyable working experience of my life; in fact I feel embarrassed calling it work. Really it simply was a labour of love. The opportunity to travel, fly in the sky, play golf, and meet terrific people was brilliant.

Thanks to all the golf course managers and professionals who allowed us to interrupt their busy schedules to play and photograph their golf courses. We really appreciate your support and trust you see the value in being part of this project.

Thanks to everyone at Funtastic, especially Lian Smith, as it was during a conversation with her that this concept was born. Also to Eric Huang for believing in the idea, and to my editor, Mat, and designer, Kar Heng—we finally got there.

To my sponsor, Ping, thanks for your support—your product is second to none.

Thanks to all the helicopter pilots for taking Richard and I up in the sky. I had never been in a helicopter before and it really was a thrill.

Thanks to my professional buddies, Stevie Howe, Tony Colless, Andrew Lowe, Matthew Cutler, Matthew Clements, James and Andrew Huddle, David and Simon Shepherd, Tarin McManus, John Hassan, Peter O'Dwyer, Sarah Anderson, and Miss Foo. Your support and knowledge has been greatly appreciated.

Finally and most importantly, a special thanks to my brilliant photographer Richard Castka—it was not a coincidence that we met mate. It was great to see a professional at work. You opened me up to a whole new creative world and I learnt so much from our experiences.

I would like to dedicate this book to my mother, Lorraine McManus, for rising through adversity.

In memory of my father, Gary McManus.

*Acknowledgement*

# Richard Castka

Richard Castka moved to Hong Kong in 1990 with his chartered civil engineer wife Gillian and two small children. Richard formed his company, Sportpix International, and soon established himself as the leading golf course and tournament photographer in the Asia region. Since then, Richard has travelled the world each year on assignment to shoot world renowned golf courses and high profile events.

Being commissioned to photograph the golf courses for *A Golfer's View* was both a tremendous opportunity and a logistical nightmare, as most of the courses were spread far and wide across the southern hemisphere.

The timing of a golf course shoot is always of critical importance because to get the very best results the work needs to be done on a well prepared golf course at the right time of day at the right time of year and in perfect weather conditions. As all of the courses featured in the book had to be shot both from the ground and from a helicopter, I should have spent much more time than usual to carry out the work. However this turned out to be practically impossible as we met rain and cloudy skies just about everywhere we went, except for sunny Queensland.

It was pouring with rain when we arrived in Sydney in mid November to shoot the stunning 18-hole golf course at New South Wales Golf Club, and it was again pouring with rain when we left there three days later without getting the helicopter into the sky. We encountered thick grey clouds and summer storms in New Zealand but somehow managed to squeeze just enough sunshine out of each location to successfully complete each of the three shoots.

I returned to Sydney at the end of January to try to complete the job we'd started almost three months earlier, and once again the rain lashed the fuselage of the plane as we taxied to the terminal building. Two days later a gap appeared in the blanket of clouds, and the helicopter was called in from the nearby international airport. One hour later the aerial shoot was complete, and five minutes after that the heavens opened as yet another huge storm lashed the area.

Having had the privilege to photograph some of the world's most prestigious golf courses over the past 15 years, I feel suitably qualified to say that the courses featured in this book are just as good as most of the courses we as amateur golfers think of as being the best in the world (the ones we regularly see on TV). See for yourself—go and play them. I completed more than 87,000 kilometres of air travel and covered over 2,500kms by road in order to photograph all of the courses. Guess what? I didn't get to play any of them!

*Acknowledgement*